W9-DEL-073

MAY 2017

Pete
the Parakeet

Mary Elizabeth Salzmann

Consulting Editor, Diane Craig, M.A./Reading Specialist

ABDO
Publishing Company

Published by ABDO Publishing Company, 4940 Viking Drive, Edina, Minnesota 55435.

Printed in the United States.

Credits
Edited by: Pam Price
Curriculum Coordinator: Nancy Tuminelly
Cover and Interior Design and Production: Mighty Media
Photo and Illustration Credits: BananaStock Ltd., Brand X Pictures, Comstock, Corbis Images, Digital Vision, Eyewire Images, Hemera, Tracy Kompelien, PhotoDisc, Stockbyte

Library of Congress Cataloging-in-Publication Data

Salzmann, Mary Elizabeth, 1968-
   Pete the Parakeet / Mary Elizabeth Salzmann.
      p. cm. -- (Rhyme time)
   Includes index.
   ISBN 1-59197-811-4 (hardcover)
   ISBN 1-59197-917-X (paperback)
   1. English language--Rhyme--Juvenile literature. I. Title. II. Rhyme time (ABDO Publishing Company)

PE1517.S356 2004
428.1'3--dc22

                                                                        2004050403

SandCastle™ books are created by a professional team of educators, reading specialists, and content developers around five essential components that include phonemic awareness, phonics, vocabulary, text comprehension, and fluency. All books are written, reviewed, and leveled for guided reading, early intervention reading, and Accelerated Reader® programs and designed for use in shared, guided, and independent reading and writing activities to support a balanced approach to literacy instruction.

Let Us Know

After reading the book, SandCastle would like you to tell us your stories about reading. What is your favorite page? Was there something hard that you needed help with? Share the ups and downs of learning to read. We want to hear from you! To get posted on the ABDO Publishing Company Web site, send us e-mail at:

sandcastle@abdopub.com

SandCastle Level: Fluent

Words that rhyme do not have to be spelled the same. These words rhyme with each other:

beat

meet

parakeet

cheat

sweet

cleat

complete

treat

feat

tweet

Michelle pretends to listen to her bear's heart **beat**.

Shelby works on her assignment until it is **complete**.

Cole keeps his eyes on his own paper during the test.

He does not **cheat**.

Amber loves the first day of school because she gets to see her friends and **meet** new kids.

Devin tightens the laces of his right baseball **cleat**.

The bird sitting on the cat's head is a **parakeet**.

The team won the championship.
They are very proud of their **feat**.

Jada likes to put honey on her pancakes to make them taste sweet.

Sometimes Leslie gets a doughnut as a special treat.

Adrian's pet bird doesn't talk.

It only says tweet.

Pete the Parakeet

This is Pete the parakeet.

Pete likes to play card games and eat.

Pete's Card Game Rule:
DO NOT CHEAT!

Pete the parakeet
really likes to win,
but he will never cheat.

16

Pete wants someone to play with, so he calls his pal Tweet and says, "Let's meet."

Tweet comes over
and takes a seat.

He wants to win, so he wears
his lucky cleat.

Pete's Card Game Rule:
DO NOT CHEAT!

Go
Fish

Pete and Tweet
play until the game is complete.

Pete's Card Game Rule:
DO NOT CHEAT!

The lucky cleat
helps Tweet beat Pete.

What a feat!

Pete's Card Game Rule:
DO NOT CHEAT!

Go Fish

Go Fish

Go Fish

The prize
is a sweet treat
that Tweet
shares with Pete!

Rhyming Riddle

What do you call a trick
performed by a small parrot?

Parakeet feat

Glossary

assignment. work given to someone to complete

cleat. a shoe with metal or rubber points on the sole to provide traction

complete. done or finished

feat. an act or deed that requires a lot of courage, strength, or skill

parakeet. a small parrot with brightly colored feathers and a long, pointed tail

About SandCastle™

A professional team of educators, reading specialists, and content developers created the SandCastle™ series to support young readers as they develop reading skills and strategies and increase their general knowledge. The SandCastle™ series has four levels that correspond to early literacy development in young children. The levels are provided to help teachers and parents select the appropriate books for young readers.

Emerging Readers
(no flags)

Beginning Readers
(1 flag)

Transitional Readers
(2 flags)

Fluent Readers
(3 flags)

These levels are meant only as a guide. All levels are subject to change.

To see a complete list of SandCastle™ books and other nonfiction titles from ABDO Publishing Company, visit www.abdopub.com or contact us at: 4940 Viking Drive, Edina, Minnesota 55435 • 1-800-800-1312 • fax: 1-952-831-1632